THE COMPA
SAMURAI LIVES ON

By
Bestselling Author
Jim Stovall

Foreword
by
Roma Klemmer

Introduction
by
Kimberly Zink

Creative Force Press

Creative Force Press

The Compassionate Samurai Lives On
© 2013 by Jim Stovall
www.klemmer.com
www.jimstovall.com

This title is also available as an eBook. Visit
www.CreativeForcePress.com/titles for more information.

Published by Creative Force Press
4704 Pacific Ave, Suite C, Lacey, WA 98503
www.CreativeForcePress.com

ISBN: 978-1-939989-07-9

Printed in the United States of America

Photo credits: Klemmer & Associates

Table of Contents

Foreword

by Roma Klemmer

I had the amazing privilege of being married to Brian Klemmer, my best friend. I learned so much from him over the 27 years we were married, about life, living from abundance, and finding forgiveness. When Brian and I met, I was a single mother of two young boys working to provide them the life I believed they deserved. Brian came into our lives, and we were a family-- no ifs, ands, or buts about it. He loved us all, unconditionally.

When he committed to something, or someone, circumstances never dictated his behavior. Balance was something he worked on throughout the years and always made sure that his family felt appreciated, loved, and supported, even when he was busy beyond belief. He practiced what he preached.

A devout Christian, he demonstrated his faith through his tithe, how he treated his children, and how amazing he was with me.

Something that inspired me about Brian was his ability to believe in people. He was always encouraging me to pursue my passions, whether it be painting or hiking. He trusted freely and forgave easily. Gossip was something that simply did not exist in his world. He lived in abundance, yet never got sucked into materialism. I can still remember him wearing sandals with socks on the beach, which totally embarrassed me, yet he was completely comfortable in his own skin.

He was passionate about reaching the world with the principles he believed in. Not only did he want to change the world, he wanted to create world changers. I believe the evidence that he achieved that goal shows throughout this book. You will read many testimonials from people who never had the chance to meet Brian Klemmer, but did not need to meet him to be enrolled in his mission.

The tools he used to change lives are exhibited within the Klemmer & Associates Workshops. These workshops are still producing remarkable results for the attendees, which keeps his vision alive and growing even after his death.

He had a heart for people and was always gently probing them to be more than they thought possible. He gave others hope to dream big, not only to radically change their own lives, but to be able to contribute to the world in a massive capacity.

Raising millions of dollars over his lifetime for different causes that he believed in was the kind of thing that got Brian truly excited. He was solution oriented, never letting himself dwell on the problem. Being a problem solver gave him the ability to network, and even create opportunities for others because of his willingness to see beyond the obvious boundaries.

Brian believed that anything is possible and that miracles do occur. That belief is instilled in me, and thousands of others, who dare to be inspired by a man with vision.

Introduction

by Kimberly Zink

Brian Klemmer was a remarkable man – not just because of his unshakable commitment to create a vision, but the breadth and depth of that vision. Most people are aware of the problems on this planet--the pain, poverty, war, disease, and despair--but few have taken responsibility as leaders to address those issues and recreate the world in a way that works for everyone, with no one left out. Brian Klemmer created that plan, a strategic 500-year plan, which he not only dreamed up and wrote about, but also invested every fiber of his being to launch. And now, after his passing, that dream continues to grow as a living legacy in the hearts of the leaders, the Compassionate Samurai, he trained. As you read their stories in this book, I know you will be inspired, and I hope you will be challenged to take your place among them, a leader in recreating this world.

Brian believed in the power of experiential training to raise people's awareness and compassion, but also to teach them practical skills to achieve their dreams and live their highest potential. It is the passion to release people into their potential through transformational work that has driven the Klemmer & Associates team for the past 20 years. Over 100,000 lives have been touched by our unique training practice. While many speakers and "training" companies offer informational seminars and "how-to books," what we do is different. It is completely immersive.

To illustrate this contrast, remember back to a foreign

language class in high school. After hours and hours of study, you may recall just a few phrases from that "informational" setting. How could you really become fluent in a foreign language though? You have to live with the people in their culture. You must become immersed. Similarly, Brian Klemmer designed environments where you can be immersed in new practices of awareness, commitment, follow-through, health, potential, connection, honesty, and achievement. He created the opportunity for you to become fluent in effective living and leadership!

Let me share what four of those carefully designed transformational environments look like...

Our Personal Mastery (PM) division is led by highly-trained, compassionate people who are committed to sharing teaching and experiences with you that will empower you to have revelation after revelation about your life and what is keeping you stuck in the holding pattern versus allowing you to land at your destination. After spending 2.5 days with us, you may see transformational results, like an increase in your income, a new awareness of what win/win thinking really is, courage to be responsible for your own success instead of being a victim to circumstances, a decrease in procrastination, the development of healthy working and personal relationships, a heightened state of activity, and a noticeable increase of love and compassion toward yourself and others – just to name a few!

Our Advanced Leadership Seminar (ALS) is all about breakthrough. You will be immersed for 5 days, focused on breaking through to your potential--the real you that the world deserves. Whether you are a Fortune 500 executive or a stay-at-home parent, you will have the opportunity to step up your game. You will be equipped with practical tools to overcome doubts, fears, and excess baggage from your past and experience a new level of clarity and assurance. Takeaways from this seminar include powerful skills for communication; awareness around trust and keeping your agreements; how to remain grounded in the face of conflict, stress, or difficult circumstances; and how to be a dynamic team leader and a contributing team player. After this 5-day, high-level leadership course, you will understand how to manage your deeply-held competing commitments and reprogram your subconscious beliefs into alignment with your values. Never again will you be able to say you are not able, or not enough.

Heart of the Samurai (Heart) is a carefully-designed, 6-day, master-level workshop where your purpose will be crystallized and you will experience the meaning of abundance and contribution. You will step into many facets of leadership and creativity, and you will be given the opportunity to surrender; not surrender to difficulties or challenges, but to the weight of your destiny. You'll understand what it means to be content and driven at the same time, and you'll see the vision of your future expand exponentially. Additionally, you will be invited into master sessions where you will be mentored by truly remarkable individuals, world shapers (people like Jim Stovall!).

Samurai Camp (Sam Camp) is a 90-day life creation challenge. You will stretch and grow to achieve goals and dreams you wouldn't have even dared to hope for at the beginning of your journey. This is the phase where "the rubber meets the road," and you get to use every transformational tool you've been practicing along the way. Prepare to be loved, coached, and supported in ways you've never imagined as you are held accountable to achieve your goals and live out your destiny in a fulfilling, balanced, connected way.

Brian was very committed to teaching adults how to grow beyond their self-imposed limitations and become Compassionate Samurai, but he was even more excited about touching young hearts. The goal? To empower the next generation with this transformational work before they even have a chance to adopt destructive beliefs. That vision is lived out in our <u>Youth Leadership Camps</u> (for teens ages 12-18) and our <u>Playful Mastery Class</u> (children ages 5-12). We are committed to empowering the entire family to move forward together!

Our corporate division extends our experiential training model into the business arena offering companies customized training systems for their leaders, managers, and front-line employees. Companies such as Suzuki Motor Company, GE, Disney, and Christi Clinic have reported measurable results from their partnership with K&A. Some of those results include moving work teams from reluctant compliance to heartfelt commitment, bursts of creative problem solving, reducing the number of meetings while increasing productivity, and accomplishing more with less while maintaining a responsible mindset.

It is the greatest honor of my life to lead the Klemmer & Associates team. I am humbled and challenged every day as we constantly look for even more effective ways to touch individual lives and influence business.

I would like to share with you that I am not just the President of K&A, I am a student of this work. Not too many years ago, I sat in a Champion's Workshop (an introductory experience we still offer in cities around the world) and heard Brian Klemmer talk about shifting belief systems and taking responsibility. I dared to believe in myself and my potential and signed up to go to Personal Mastery. If you met me today you might not understand what a stretch that was for me to even hope for myself to have a future. I was obese, relationally challenged, and shame-filled. I wasn't just broke, I was over $90K dollars in debt. From a young age, I had suffered unspeakable abuse, both emotionally and sexually, and I was living out my victim story in an endless cycle of self-defeat. But something that night in the workshop resonated deep inside my heart, and I just *knew*.

I went straight through all four levels of the Klemmer training in 6 months. After just 18 months of practicing these principles, I had created a net worth of over 300k, I released 80 lbs., and met and married my best friend! This journey hasn't always been easy, but it has been worth it. I'm not special--I just dared to follow my heart, believe in myself and take action! If I can live my dreams, anyone (including you) can.

I have a favor to ask of you, as you read the stories in this book: read between the lines. The lines of text on these pages speak of actions, results, and feelings. But I invite you to look deeper--past the obvious. See the hope, faith, love, joy, passion, commitment, acceptance, and discipline that were the driving forces behind the actions that created the results.

As the President of Klemmer & Associates, I am personally committed to continue the Legacy that Brian Klemmer began over

20 years ago. Each and every one of our trainers, coaches, and support staff is committed to building bold, ethical leaders who create a world that works for everyone with no one left out. You will not find a more professional, ethical, committed, and contributive gathering of leaders anywhere. We look forward to supporting you as you take bold action along your own destiny journey!

1

Triumph Over Tragedy

We go through our lives trying to attract good things and avoid bad things. However, when we look at the great things we are experiencing today in a historical perspective, we often find that they began in tragedy.

One of the many great things I get to do in my life is speak to millions of people in arena events and business conventions around the world. I remember a number of years ago, just before the dawning of the new millennium, I was speaking at an outdoor amphitheater in Maui, Hawaii, for a group of international businesspeople. The backstage area was little more than a path through a beautiful garden surrounded by a tropical rainforest. The stage backed up to a picturesque lagoon with the ocean waves breaking on the reef in the distance. The crowd was seated in a bowl-shaped amphitheater with rows of theater seats stretching up the mountainside.

As I stood there preparing myself mentally for a one-hour speech, I remembered a time in my life when this would have seemed impossible to me. I had lost my sight at age 29 and had not yet figured out how to cope with life as a blind person. I moved into a small room in the back of my house where I gathered my radio, my telephone, and my tape recorder. I really fully intended to *never* leave the 9- by 12-foot sanctuary of my little room.

My recollections were interrupted by rousing music as the master of ceremonies introduced me.

"In spite of blindness, Jim Stovall has been a National Olympic weightlifting champion, a successful investment broker, the President of the Emmy Award-winning Narrative Television Network, and a highly sought-after author and platform speaker. He is the author of 25 books, and four of his books have been made into major motion pictures.

"Steve Forbes, president and CEO of *Forbes* Magazine, says, 'Jim Stovall is one of the most extraordinary men of our era.'

"For his work in making television accessible to our nation's 13 million blind and visually impaired people, The President's Committee on Equal Opportunity selected Jim Stovall as Entrepreneur of the Year. Jim Stovall has been featured in *The Wall Street Journal*, *Forbes* Magazine, *USA Today*, and has been seen on *Good Morning America*, *CNN*, and *CBS Evening News*. He was also chosen as the International Humanitarian of the Year, joining Jimmy Carter, Nancy Reagan, and Mother Teresa as recipients of this honor."

As I climbed onto the stage to thunderous applause, I thought of the tragedy that had put me in that little room and the triumph that had brought me to this stage. Little did I know that the triumph was still unfolding as there was a very special man in the audience that day named Brian Klemmer.

Several months later, Brian called me and told me he had been in the audience in Hawaii, and he invited me to speak at a training event he was having in San Diego for several hundred people. I told him my outrageous fee, and that I generally spoke for many thousands of people.

Brian was somewhere between persistent and tenacious, so I agreed to try it one time. That began a relationship that lasted over a decade until his untimely death, and has brought me in front of Klemmer audiences dozens of times since.

Writing books or making speeches, when done properly, can change the lives of people. But when you have a fertile audience such as you find at a Klemmer event, you have an opportunity to change the world changers.

I had been speaking for Brian Klemmer events several times a year for a decade, and as we were preparing to leave for another Klemmer event, I got the fateful call. Brian Klemmer had suddenly and unexpectedly died. I made the obligatory calls and sent notes and flowers as expected, and even recorded a segment for Brian's memorial service; but it didn't seem to be enough.

I struggled with what kind of lasting honor or tribute would be appropriate to commemorate the impactful life of someone like Brian Klemmer. Then it dawned on me. Brian's legacy remains and continues to grow in the lives of those he touched.

I am privileged to share just a handful of those impacted lives with you in the pages of this book.

I remember when my friend, Michael Fenner, called looking for a transition in his life. He was considering going to an arena event held by one of my colleagues in the personal development field. While I have great respect for this colleague, I knew Michael Fenner was in need of a dose of Brian Klemmer.

Michael dipped his toe into the Klemmer world, and shortly, found himself totally immersed and changed.

I was a man in my early 50s who was struggling. I was distraught, confused and not sure how I was going to address all of the issues in my life. I was concerned mostly with how I was going to change others so that it would meet my needs.

My close friend, Jim Stovall, suggested that I do some research on Klemmer & Associates. Jim had been a speaker for one of Brian Klemmer's seminars for a few years and had introduced me to the information a while back, but I was now open to hearing more. I took up his suggestion and was intrigued enough to attend Klemmer & Associates' first level adult program, Personal Mastery, in October 2011. Personal Mastery showed me that I have a voice and need to use it. I realized that by me choosing to step up that weekend and do something different, I was not only helping myself but also helping others find their voice.

I continued into the second level of the program, Advanced Leadership, and it was there that I was guided on a path of recognition; a path of discovering who I am and who I want to be. I discovered that I rock, and that I have acquired many gifts throughout the years that I needed to share with others. I am now open to talk about my past, and I am able to trust and know that I will not be judged on what happened to me. I learned to love and accept myself. I was able to free myself of the pain I carried for years. Instead of seeing myself as a victim when I tell my story, I now use my past as a source of strength to impact others who have faced the same occurrences in their life.

The third level program, Heart of the Samurai, is where I expanded and strengthened my beliefs in myself. I have learned to live in the moment, treat others with respect, and love. I realized it is okay not to be perfect. There will be failures and setbacks, but quitting and not trying my best is not an option in life. I now take the time to be open to what others are going through. I know how to hold them and myself accountable. I have come away from 'Heart' knowing that I can be trusted as a leader in the community. I am a product of Brian Klemmer's legacy, and because of that, I am creating my own. I am a bold, focused, responsible, and abundant man. I did not believe that before. Klemmer has taught me that I, and only I, can make choices for my own life. I can create whatever I believe is necessary to pursue life with a purpose. That purpose is to bring love, compassion, and strength to others.

Strength and a voice—I have always known I had them but Klemmer helped me acknowledge and grab hold of them. Since Heart of the Samurai, I have given much more of myself to others. I volunteered as a staff member at Klemmer's Youth Leadership Camp where I realized I was living my dream, encouraging youth.

My son died suddenly November 25th of 2012. Words would not do justice to the pain and confusion I felt at the loss of my son. What I do believe is that because of Brian Klemmer and the work he started, I am able to grieve and support my family to grieve through this tragic loss in a healthy way. Klemmer has shown me that I can make choices, and I chose to use his life and death to bring courage, strength, and most importantly love to others. I have chosen to take my experiences, both good and bad, and use them as gifts to others.

Because of Klemmer & Associates, I know my purpose in life is to bring love, compassion, and strength to others.

I am a bold, focused, responsible and abundant man.

Live and love life with a purpose.

Michael D. Fenner

All of us approach our goals and our destiny as mountain climbers at the base of a daunting peak. It is difficult enough to reach the summit unencumbered, but I meet countless people around the world who are trying to climb their mountain while carrying guilt and burdens from their past.

The simplest thing and the most difficult thing you may ever accomplish is to lay these burdens down, and let the guilt go.

Carrie Collingridge found the secret to this challenge through Klemmer & Associates.

I attended a Klemmer Personal Mastery seminar in October of 2012, in Kamloops, BC. What I got from that weekend has changed my life forever, and for the better! Through Klemmer, I was able to work through a lot of past situations that had been holding me back from my dreams and passions.

My dad took his own life when I was a child, and through Klemmer, I was able to realize and acknowledge that it was not my fault, and it did not mean that he did not love me. His death was not about me. I was able to forgive him. This had been crippling me since his death, and now I am free and at peace with it. I realized that failed romantic relationships that I had experienced were not about my self-worth, but rather just about poor choices. I have been living with social anxiety my whole life, and for a long time, I allowed it to control me. This is a condition that is not meant to define me, and I will no longer let it hold me back in life. I realized that I am not a victim of life, but that I do have control over the life I want to live. I have a choice. Whether I see it coming or not, it is my decisions that lead me to where I end up.

Klemmer & Associates has supported me in having a vision and making a plan. I expect that there will be trials. I will deal with them as they come, and I choose to keep going. As long as I have a goal and stay focused, it is okay if things do not always go how I expect them to. I will enjoy the journey, because life takes place in the getting there. I have learned to take responsibility for the choices I have made and where they have led me in life, good and bad. I choose to take the hurt in life and turn it into strength and a positive attitude. I choose to live a life with purpose, meaning, and enjoyment. I choose to make something out of my life and of myself.

Personal Mastery has helped me focus on what is important in my life. Most of what I stress over is not important enough to allow myself to become overwhelmed and to interrupt my life. Despite the things that I have suffered through, there are far more things that I have not suffered, and I am grateful for all the good that I do have in life. Through Klemmer, I started working toward a doctorate degree, and am currently at the master level. This has been my life passion, and I will succeed.

Carrie Collingridge

Erica Hunt found the key to triumph over tragedy, through a Klemmer event, that prepared her for the ultimate challenge of life and death.

In 2009, I had an experience with an individual that sent me spiraling into the abyss of doubt and depression. I was frustrated. I thought I had worked through those emotions of anger and frustration, but apparently I had not. My mind wandered back to a book written by a man named Brian Klemmer "If How-To's Were Enough...." This book caught my attention because it gave practical and insightful ways to work through the daily challenges of life most of us face any given day. He discussed how to deal with challenges of self-doubt, seeing value in oneself and, most importantly, ways to develop a personal calling/purpose in this life. In the back of the book there was a promotion for a hands-on seminar called Personal Mastery. Little did I know Brian Klemmer's Personal Mastery was not only going to set me free from the things that were holding me back, but it was going to lay the groundwork and prepare me for the biggest challenge of my life. I chose to follow the path Klemmer & Associates set and took several other Klemmer seminars that same year.

In the midst of it all, my husband and I were blessed with a last minute addition to our family, our only baby girl, Ella Lanay Hunt. We rejoiced in her birth; however, within a few months we were in despair as we received the devastating news; our 4-month-old, Ella, had a terminal disease, SMA, and we were told to go home and hold her. She would die in our arms or in our sleep. In this moment, we chose to take her home to live, not to die. We chose not to mourn her death while she still had life here on this earth. We went home with true intention to make lasting memories with our daughter.

From the very beginning of our walk down the road of "living *with a child with a terminal illness," EVERYTHING from my experiences with Klemmer & Associates were being put into full effect. Without this company and the life skills they teach, I know our future would have looked very different. I don't know that I would have had the courage to choose life for our family, for Ella. Klemmer taught me to embrace others and accept their love and support. Klemmer taught me to just "be" and stop pushing to make things look the way I wanted. Klemmer taught me to accept and love myself for who God made me. Klemmer taught me to be true to my intentions and realize my commitment to areas of change and growth in my life. Most importantly, Klemmer reminded me of why we are here...to give and receive love.*

As we continue to journey through this disease and diagnosis, we are living fuller and without apprehension. We are experiencing life to its fullest EVERY DAY. Tomorrow may come, or maybe it won't for us, but that's okay; it is for today that we live. Klemmer & Associates has changed countless lives, including mine. I am sincerely grateful and pray for the continued growth of Klemmer & Associates' training efforts worldwide.

Erica Hunt
Mary Kay Sales Director

Literally hours before I was to leave for another Klemmer & Associates event, I received the call that Brian Klemmer had died. I sat in my office in total shock.

My first thought was of the loss of my friend and fellow traveler on the road of success. Next, I thought about the looming training event and assumed it would be cancelled. However, when I found out people in Australia and New Zealand were already en-route to the Klemmer event in San Diego, I asked myself, "What would Brian Klemmer do?"

I could hear the voice of my friend saying, "Do what you were put here to do, and remember, it's not about you."

I continue to do Klemmer events, and his impact continues to grow.

This book is not a historical document designed to recount someone's past. It is, instead, a challenge for you and me to continue to grow and develop into the future.

2

The Business of Life

Other than our name, the work we do is how we define ourselves and others around us. Sometimes, the difference between success in business and failure in business is a thin margin. The change we're looking for is not in the economy or the business world. It is inside of us.

Bryan Penrod found the change he was looking for in his business and his life.

I had been hearing for months how countless Associates and top USANA Fortune 25 leaders were experiencing new levels of "Revolutionary Transformation" in their USANA businesses, families, and other personal areas of their lives from attending Klemmer & Associates trainings. I decided to check it out for myself, and what I saw...was impressive. If you can no longer afford "poverty" or "less than adequate" relationships with others, make sure you do not miss out on the next Klemmer event.

Bryan Penrod
2-Star Diamond Director, USANA Presidents Award Recipient
2005

Change in business and life begins from the point where we are, not where we wish to be. We must be honest about our current condition and how we got there, so we can move toward where we want and deserve to be.

Dave Schedin found this breakthrough at a Klemmer event.

My life dramatically changed after a 28-year marriage ended. I found myself alone and living a life I did not desire. I knew I was here by choices I had made, and some choices I did not make. My business was on the edge and all my other relationships were shallow. I was alone. God used K&A as part of my recovery, not just getting back on my feet, but for creating changes and shifts inside myself that allowed me to make choices that moved me forward. Klemmer & Associates helped me get unstuck. Applying the principles of what I learned in ALL levels of the Klemmer trainings, I have a renewed heart that is in a deeply committed, and what I call, a Level 10 relationship. My business is growing, and I have recently added two strategic partners who are helping it grow substantially.

One K&A training module alone allowed the company to make another $150,000 in just 5 months! I can now see opportunities I've never seen before, and I owe it to being led to Klemmer & Associates' training. It has also helped my coaching business and my clients create greater results. Having the opportunity to go back and staff the workshops is a powerful opportunity and provides for continued growth. Staffing Samurai Camp is the best leadership training you can get on this planet!

"Klemmer & Associates training is not just something you should do...it is something you deserve!"

Dave Schedin

CEO, CompuTrek Automotive Management Systems

Suzanne Lukasievich is one of the countless people who didn't get a chance to meet Brian Klemmer before his death, but her success keeps his legacy alive.

In 2010 I was laid off. After I had postponed attending the two upper-level trainings of Klemmer & Associates for some time, I immediately re-committed to attending Heart of the Samurai (and later Samurai Camp). It was only a couple of days before Brian Klemmer died. The father figure I had never met passed away before I could meet him. I was heartbroken, and quickly understood the importance of living each day to the fullest and having a sense of urgency in what I do.

Through Klemmer, I have learned to speak up for myself to obtain the proper wage for the positions I currently command (administration and property management), and to expand the work I do along with the budget base. In one challenge, I created over $12,000.00 in one month. I plan to double my current income by next year. I also have expanded the services I offer at assisted living facilities. I do network marketing with a corporation that is over 50 years old, and enjoy the many benefits they offer, like traveling and enjoying the business aspects.

Suzanne Lukasievich

Oftentimes, comfort keeps us from achieving excellence. No one ever forced people out of their comfort zone like my friend Brian

Klemmer.

Before I had experienced Klemmer, I was financially stable. However, I wanted to provide more and have the means to do more. Through the Klemmer Seminars, I was able to push myself and my mind beyond boundaries that I had created, which, in turn, exposed how capable I really am. I created $91,500 in 3 months, in addition to what I normally earn in that time period.

Samuel Gbadebo

Jeff Sutherlin used his experience with Klemmer & Associates to go from good to better, and the best is still to come.

I am an owner of one of the largest real estate agencies in Phoenix: United Brokers Group, with 200 associates. When I first started taking the Klemmer classes, I was lacking direction. I was also thinking small. I had a strong skill set and track record, but I didn't truly embrace the opportunities that were in front of me. I lacked clarity. Klemmer & Associates programs allowed me to leave my negative baggage behind so I could move forward with confidence and a clear conscience. I have had a lot of training in leadership and I have received mentoring from some of the best in the world, but nothing has ever had the impact that Klemmer's programs have had on me. Since I went through the curriculum, I have never looked back.

Jeff Sutherlin
United Brokers Group
President, MBA, Associate Broker, and Co-founder

Mary Sullivan found, through her Klemmer experience, that the key to viewing the present and the future is sometimes as simple as looking in the mirror and deciding who we are and where we want to go.

I started really hiding the true me after some emotional experiences in my corporate life and my first business venture. I didn't realize that I was wearing a mask and hiding out.

In the past, I was always a helper. Not only helping others with problems, but even taking on their problems. I got overloaded. I stopped reaching out to my friends because I was afraid their problems would break me. I live and work with very intense personalities. Before I attended Klemmer seminars, I was constantly being run over. I didn't realize that I was avoiding going after my own accomplishments; I never set a goal that I didn't KNOW I could meet.

My Klemmer experiences helped me realize that "not feeling worthy" was holding me back. I now know that I am worthy; I deserve great success. Setting goals that stretch me is now fun instead of frightening, because I can see that so much more is possible. The opinions of others no longer influence my goals or my success. Now, since attending the Klemmer training, I am called the "cat herder extraordinaire" because I lead with calmness and confidence. Co-workers not only listen to me, they seek out my opinion. We actually get things done now. Ideas aren't just discussed, they are implemented and our business is exploding.

With the experiences I have had through Klemmer, I now know that it really can be as quick as making a choice; I chose to return to the authentic me. I am now seeking out the fun in life, and fun people. My current relationships with family and friends are deeper and more meaningful. Klemmer taught me that I don't need to own the problems of others to support them. Now, I can help them look at the issue differently, to clearly see, and to love themselves. Not only do I support others better, I am taking better care of myself. As life happens around me, I now choose how I let it affect my life. Suffering is truly optional.

Mary Sullivan

Bill and Kathy Hellwig experienced the group dynamic of Brian Klemmer's training. One of the most exciting things about the road to success is the people you get to travel with.

During the past 9 years, most of our personal network marketing team has experienced the Klemmer & Associates courses. We credit K&A's personal leadership development and transformational training for our phenomenal success. Four of our team leaders have earned over one million dollars so far, for a combined estimated income exceeding $7 million dollars as a result...definitely worth the price of tuition!

Personally, we have met some of our closest friends through the courses, and have been fortunate to become friends with many of the Klemmer & Associates staff, including Brian Klemmer. Our adult children experienced the courses, and our family dynamic has been greatly enhanced. As a result, we have chosen to re-visit several courses to staff or audit. Our relationship with the Lord was re-kindled through friendships developed during Advanced Leadership, Heart of the Samurai, and Sam Camp. As a result, we have been leading a local ministry since 2006.

Klemmer & Associates continues to be a blessing to us in all areas of our life.

Bill and Kathy Hellwig
Colorado Springs, CO

Nancy Rinard was able to apply Klemmer & Associates training to her business immediately in very practical and real ways.

The information I gained while taking the outstanding Klemmer & Associates Network Marketing Webinar Series has already successfully impacted my USANA Health Science business and has given me many keys to further build my business.

The weekly coaching tips were powerful and were exactly what I needed to hear to propel my business from one level to another. Through S.M.A.R.T. goal setting and then analyzing my goals, I noticed feelings of fear and risk, but was still motivated to plunge forward and take on the challenge with boldness and urgency. In less than one week, I had 17 people listening to a presentation in my home resulting in new registrations.

My biggest take-away was learning to focus on what my prospects need and show them the benefits I can offer through USANA.

In addition, I have listened to several of the downloads that are available with the webinar registration, and found them very motivational and useful.

Nancy Rinard
Director – USANA Health Sciences

Paul takes us on his Klemmer journey from prison to prosperity and beyond.

I started attending seminars through Klemmer & Associates in April of 2012. My intention to start the seminars came with the hope of simply creating more finances in my life through a possible new business venture. What I actually found was so much more. I found myself. I discovered that I am capable of creating amazing abundance in my life, and in the lives of others, in a very short amount of time. Yes, I created it--no one did it for me. However, I have never been alone in the process.

What perhaps is the most remarkable part of this journey for me is that I had actually been incarcerated for over 8 years for living life on my terms without any consideration for others. I was released from prison in 2009 and came into the community with $600 to my name, no job, no housing, and only a small circle of friends who weren't incarcerated. I worked for temp labor at minimum wage for 11 months before getting my first full-time job. I mowed lawns, demo'd construction sites with a sledge hammer, and yes, even dug ditches...

I started Klemmer seminars without traveling much prior, living a fairly routine lifestyle, earning about $2,000 per month. Since going through Klemmer, I have created $7000 in one week through my business. I've flown thousands of miles and continue to travel nearly every month for both vacation and invitation-only speaking engagements...of which I am the speaker! I have been invited to be a contributing author to an international trade magazine in my industry. In a single week, I created my first art show of oil paintings that now hangs in a recognized gallery. One week I didn't have *canvases or an easel, and the next week I had large paintings hanging in a gallery with visitors, wine, and live music to open the show. I've volunteered dozens of hours in my community, passed an exam for my pilots' license, and completed many, many other goals. Next week, I'm going skydiving with several friends--just because I can.*

I used to believe that I could only create hundreds of dollars, have a small circle of friends, and was pretty much destined to have my life look like it did for my parents. Now I think in thousands and tens of thousands of dollars, I have a massive circle of friends of which I think I've lost count, and play life big...which I believe is how I was created to play in this life. In my experience, the heart of Klemmer & Associates is in the friends and facilitators that are also living life full-out, full-on with the intention to create goodness in the world through leadership from the heart, The Heart of the Compassionate Samurai.

I am a Forgiving, Successful, Adorable, and Adventurous Man, Full of God's Understanding, Love, and Life

Paul, U.S.A.

Brian Klemmer's lessons helped Regina Manasan go from simply making a living to creating a life.

My journey with Klemmer & Associates began in January 2012. At the time, I had an okay relationship with my husband who I had been married to for a year and a half. I had a steady 9 to 5 job, but not much of a career. I started with Klemmer thinking I could gain more confidence in the workplace and increase my income. More than that, I've increased and experienced growth in every aspect of my life. I now have an open, connected, intimate and loving relationship with my husband, who I just adore. I quit my job in June 2012 and partnered with my husband in running his business. As a result, our company's gross revenue nearly tripled from the year before, with a majority of the income earned during the latter part of last year. Most importantly, I wake up each morning feeling happier and more grateful. I am so blessed each day to live MY life because it's the one that I've created.

    Regina Manasan

Peggy Chase found the Klemmer Experience too good to keep to herself, so she gave it to her colleagues and associates.

I became the President and CEO of TERROS, Inc. in October, 2011. TERROS has partnered with Klemmer & Associates, providing Corporate Personal Mastery and Corporate Advanced Leaderships. I am so excited to share that we have over 300 of our 440 employees who have completed PM and over 110 employees who have completed ALS. I was privileged to spend a week with four of my favorite people, Kimberly Zink, John Edwards, Scott Pullan, and Kathy Fairbanks the last week of April!! The volunteers who staff our ALS were amazing.

    We have already seen tremendous positive change within our company. Employees are amazed that we would invest in them personally. I share with them that by investing in them, I am investing in our company, since they are TERROS. Our TERROS vision is "Inspiring Change for Life." Our Klemmer partnership inspires our employees to Change for Life!! We love the Klemmer team.

    Peggy Chase

John Machart also demonstrates that the best experiences are those that we share with those around us.

I will definitely recommend the Klemmer & Associates Webinar Series to other Direct Marketers...and I would not hesitate to bring another fresh group of associates to do this again.
John Machart
USANA

During my decade-long relationship with Brian Klemmer, including spending many hours discussing his business and mine, we came to understand that success and wealth are the natural result of serving others, and, therefore, mediocrity is the most selfish pursuit of any human being. Business is the vehicle through which we can give ourselves away and create value for others.

3

Relationships

There are few people who will read this book who have ever been as financially impoverished as I have been, and there are few people who read this book who have ever enjoyed more wealth than I do today. Only through becoming financially successful did I fully realize that my wealth is not a calculation of the money I have, but instead, it is made up of the caliber of my friends and the depth of the special relationships in my life.

Daniel Ashurst, through his Klemmer experience, found that we cannot love anyone until we first love ourselves.

It has been my experience, prior to Klemmer & Associates, that relationships were hard, most often ending in disappointment, and that I was not qualified, nor worthy, of a quality relationship. Through the work of K&A, and with the support of all the amazing people involved in this great work, I received the ability to trust in people. After such painful relationships in the past, I have opened my life up to be with someone. I came into Klemmer classes with the expectation of expediency – In Brian Klemmer's own words: "A large amount of change in a short amount of time." Klemmer has built an environment where people who have the desire to move and change can see quick and appropriate results. This is exactly what I have received. In October of this past year, I set the goal of getting married by the end of 2014. I was already dating someone I cared deeply about, but was very afraid to commit. Following the direction of my K&A leaders, I was able to make choices and embrace a life of trust and intimacy that far exceeds my expectations. No, not a knee-jerk reaction, but a well thought-out and rewarding relationship. My wife and I were married on January 27th, 2013. The blessings and rewards of being open and intimate have been life-changing to say the least.

Daniel Ashurst

Brian Klemmer understood that every area of life, including relationships, can always be improved. The Hoeft family embraced Brian's teachings and went from good to best.

My journey with Klemmer & Associates began in November of 2011. My husband and I had a strong marriage and, overall, life was great. A friend recommended that I go to Personal Mastery based on her positive experience. I asked my husband to join me. He was a bit skeptical, but decided to go. We were both blown away after the weekend. Since going to Personal Mastery, our marriage is a 10+, where before it was a 7 or 8. We communicate and engage with each other at a more intimate and higher level. We are both living with an abundant mindset instead of a mindset of scarcity, and our businesses have both grown with less effort. We are setting goals and dreaming like never before!

We received so much value from Personal Mastery that we

chose to move on to Advanced Leadership. We learned so much about ourselves and why we do the things we do. After experiencing all the benefits of Advanced, we wanted this for our 13-year-old son. We had a bit of a combative relationship with him at the time. We learned about Youth Leadership Camp and decided to send our son. He came back a renewed young man. With the positive changes in all of us, we now have a loving, fun and respectful relationship with our son, and he is stepping into the wonderful qualities we always knew he had! Our entire family life is completely different than when we began our Klemmer journey, so much more joy, love and fun in our family! I can't say enough good things about the workshops and the people affiliated with Klemmer & Associates!

Stacey Hoeft

Jayce Tohline learned through Klemmer & Associates that all relationships begin with ourselves. If I can't be honest and open with me, I don't have a chance of relating that way with anyone else.

In a span of 10 months, my wife and I attended all of the Klemmer & Associates personal development courses. Each step in the process helped me discover more about the "real" me. The most important testimony of change came from my adult children. They individually have pulled my wife aside to ask her what happened to me. They've noticed a tremendous change for the better, particularly in my patience in stress-filled situations. As a result, I have a closer relationship with each one of them. That alone was worth the time and money.

Jayce Tohline

Deb Damron discovered, through the lessons of my friend Brian, that the whole world can fall in love with us right after we fall in love with ourselves.

When I started my Klemmer journey a year-and-a-half ago, little did I know that I would be able to create everything I had been dreaming of my whole life. I was living a mediocre life, always wanting more and not knowing why I didn't have it. I went to motivational seminars, read books, and I was still in the same little bubble. I attended my first Klemmer course in December of 2011, and at that point, I hit the ground running, completing all of the courses within the year. When I started, I was not sure it would work, and then I had an experience that changed the way I thought about who I was.

As I went through more of the courses, I experienced more of me, and how I view who I am as a person. I was able to change my behaviors and to think differently. I used to see myself as unworthy, which justified my belief that I did not deserve to have the things I wanted. Now I see myself as a worthy woman who is deserving of all I have and more. Since taking part in the Klemmer & Associates trainings, I took a marriage that was a solid 7 and transformed it into a marriage that is now a 10 on a scale of 1-10. My relationship with my 5 children is stronger, and I have written a full feature movie that will go into production this year. Look out world...here I come! This worthy, audacious and captivating woman is here to stay!

Deb Damron

Brian Klemmer believed that information and learning are only valid if they lead to permanent change. Sally Robinson discovered this to be true.

I had spent 20 years telling the story of my marriage. I lived as a victim of circumstances that had transpired on my honeymoon! During the Personal Mastery class, I had an opportunity to experience telling my story differently. For the first time in 20 years, I realized that I had a choice in how I think about my marriage. It was the first of many "Ah-ha!" moments, and it was mind-blowing! This was the beginning of a transformation.

My husband and I had spent hundreds of hours and thousands of dollars on marital counseling, seminars, videos, retreats, and a marriage communication course, all offered by well-known organizations and individuals. These produced limited and temporary improvement in our relationship. My husband had a heart attack two weeks before our Personal Mastery weekend, but he still decided to attend with me. This was the turning point in our relationship. Personal Mastery and the workshops that followed gave us a new vocabulary to use when talking through our problems, and we began to learn how to create win/win solutions instead of playing the same old worn-out blame game.

One lesson in particular from Personal Mastery, applied over time, was THE key in healing our marriage. It was the lesson about sunglasses. God gave me added insight about this one that helped me change how I responded to my husband. This led to the breakthrough in our marriage that we had long prayed for. I know we've only just begun living in peace together, renewing our friendship and feeling satisfied in our marriage. We recently enjoyed our 25th wedding anniversary! Klemmer training was the game-changer that God used to work a miracle for us.

    Sally Robinson

Rowel Manasan found a way to reach and relate to his daughter through the teaching and training of my friend, Brian Klemmer. There can be no greater gift nor lasting legacy.

My experience with Klemmer & Associates has been absolutely amazing. For me, the most precious gift a father could hope for is the love, respect, and affection of a daughter. Before my work with Klemmer, my relationship with my daughter was distant. But after attending all four seminars, and my own daughter's attendance at Youth Leadership Camp, we have a closeness and connection that is absolutely priceless.

    Rowel Manasan

Bill Martin shows us all through his Klemmer experience that personal development is the fastest and best way to build personal relationships.

I first became aware of Klemmer & Associates in early 2011. Going to Personal Mastery that summer was most revealing; I thought I knew where my life was headed. I soon discovered that I was like a rudderless ship, going in whatever direction the winds and waves took me. Personal Mastery and the subsequent Advanced Leadership Seminar gave me the tools to see what I was doing to my life. The choices I had made up to that point had resulted in my marriage ending, depression, and a cynical attitude toward life in general. My personal relationship with my children was not where I wanted it to be, and as a divorced man, I had no confidence in starting another relationship.

Today, I am in a relationship with a woman that is more personally fulfilling and emotionally stable than I have ever known. My communication now comes from the heart. I am more open and trusting with her and with myself. My children have noticed changes in my attitude and behavior with them, and have asked me what caused the changes. I told them I had learned from Klemmer the way to stay on a path of positive change. It was a lot of hard work; change always is. But it was well worth it. Today I am less judgmental, more accepting of others, and more focused on living a worthy life. I see opportunities where I didn't before, and am more open to living out of my comfort zone. I like the person I have become and will continue learning and growing.

I am a Trusting, Surrendered and Bold Man
Bill Martin

Through bold and candid training, Klemmer & Associates teaches people to "never say never."

I was divorced over 12 years ago. I was a "lone rangerette" and vowed to never re-marry. Through the process with Klemmer & Associates, and with much trepidation, I entered into the dating arena. In two months, I had experienced over 12 dates. I am now in a relationship with a godly man of my heart's desire, and am discovering what a true loving relationship is.

As a result of experiencing the seminars with Klemmer &

Associates, I have developed strong, open, honest relationships with my children, my friends, co-workers, and business associates. I am being vulnerable, open, honest, focused, and transparent. I dare to ask the difficult questions and speak truth, yet I know that I cannot ask those questions without first asking them of myself and discovering the answers.

Suzanne Lukasievich

Teresa Clark reminds us all that the first step to learning and growth is admitting what we don't know and coming to grips with not being where we want to be.

Most people knew me as being very direct and even intimidating. I butted heads even with those close to me. I had a need to appear as one of the smartest people in the room. I thought this was the only way to gain influence, to show people how strong I was, and get my way. My adult son and I knew we loved each other, but other family members didn't even like to be around us. The funny thing is we thought that we had a great relationship! I was amazed to realize that I don't know what I don't know.

After my Klemmer experiences, my relationships improved significantly. I am developing deeper relationships instead of the superficial ones I had. I learned the value of being vulnerable and to see the value in other people's opinions. I have even dramatically increased my sales because of my new communication style.

My relationship with my son greatly improved; we are no longer fighting every day. We still have disagreements, but it no longer escalates into an argument because we now have new ways of communicating with each other. We shared a suite at one of the seminars and everyone was surprised we didn't kill each other. It brought tears to my eyes when, while making plans for the next seminar, my son asked to room with me because he felt it would be less stressful for him. I cannot explain how it feels when my adult child asks my advice and really values my opinion.

I have attended many other seminars, and I always left with the "seminar high" full of good intentions, but never followed through to make a change. I am very blessed to have friends that have enough influence that insisted I go to Klemmer. The experience was so different from past seminars, and months later, I am still practicing and using what I learned about myself. So if you are not ready for a really big change in your life, please don't go.

TC Teresa Clark

Bob Clark learned, through his Klemmer experience, that relating to others through strength does not mean beating them down; it means pulling them up.

I was a political consultant and took delight in the damage I did to my opponents. I was barbaric; I would hack and slash and destroy as much as possible. That lifestyle was not good for long-term relationships or my health. Klemmer taught me that I can be a Compassionate Samurai and still be effective at my job. I can now influence situations and get things done without being a jerk.

I used to fight with my mother all the time, as most young adults do. It was so bad that we would get into a fight and four days later she would come over and fill up my cupboards with food by way of an apology. In the last 2 months, we have had only one fight that lasted about one minute; we both caught ourselves and laughed.

It really bugged me that no one would share the details of the seminars; so much so, that I almost didn't go. The Klemmer seminars are like the movie "The Sixth Sense." If you knew the ending, it would ruin the experience.

Bob Clark

Through my relationship with Brian Klemmer, I got to speak before thousands of people from many countries, cultures, faiths, and walks of life. The more I experience people who are different, the more I realize we are all the same. Andrea and Jonathan Morris from Western Australia demonstrate this.

We are so grateful for all that we have been able to create in our lives since our involvement with Klemmer & Associates. Because of the discoveries we made, we choose to live and love powerfully, and to continue to move forward as husband and wife. Klemmer gave us the tools to open doors to create greater visions.

Andrea and Jonathan Morris
Western Australia

My relationship with Brian Klemmer, lasting over a decade, involved being a friend, a colleague, a business associate, a teacher, a student, a mentor, a mentee, a challenger, as well as being someone greatly challenged. I am pleased to see his influence continuing to affect relationships among people all around the world.

4

Bigger and Better

As a friend and colleague of mine, Brian Klemmer was always excited for me about every victory in my business and personal life. But unlike most other people, Brian always tempered his applause with encouragement to try harder, do more, be more.

I remember him reading one of my books that had been turned into a movie and telling me, "I think this is the best work on the written page and movie screen that you have done to date."

I had barely uttered a "Thank you" before Brian added, "However, I think this is far from the best work you can do. Someday, this project won't even make your top five."

Paul Jensen discovered the same thing from his Klemmer experience in that anything less than your best is just not good enough, and maybe what you think is your best today may be better tomorrow.

Of the myriad lessons I have learned from Klemmer & Associates, the one that stands above all the rest is the size of the game I am now playing. I believe I was fully engaged before, but now I see myself operating at new levels that I could only dream about early on. The fact that I can look back from this rarified level and be mildly embarrassed at what I thought was "full out" leads me to understand that one day I will be able to look back on this place from an even higher level! That's exciting!

    Paul Jensen

Through his Klemmer experience, Ray found out that success, sobriety, and life itself has to be faced one day at a time.

The value I gained from the Klemmer seminars was renewed confidence. I developed an overall kinder, gentler outlook toward people and life in general. Through the process, I was able to make some progress fighting an addiction I had been facing for some time. While the K&A work is no substitute for a formal 12-step program (K&A has never promoted itself as such a program), it certainly provided the catalyst to start that important journey. During Sam Camp, I was able to complete 56 days of sobriety and that gave me enough clarity to achieve both the goals I had set for myself during that time (camp 18).

It also gave me enough "recuperation" to realize that this was the key issue and problem I needed to face and achieve victory over. As addiction specialists say, addictions lead to either: 1. insanity, 2. incarceration, or 3. death--and not necessarily in that order. I was heading for trouble, and while I sort of knew that before attending a Champion's Workshop, I had no clue how tough it would be to fight this addiction or how spiritual the journey would need to be. Through the Klemmer work, I discovered that it was about results and not excuses or stories. The journey helped me get to a 12-step program probably years before I would have otherwise. It might have kept me out of jail, for which I'm grateful.

There were many professional benefits as well, of course things like increased punctuality and a crisper edge at work, to name a few. I was even able to turn around my performance in an internship I was participating in at work between attending ALS and Heart. I earned a positive recommendation from the internship program director, which lead to a rewarding job with a group that had very high standards. I am in my 4th year in the position. There have been ups and downs in that job (and in life) since 2009, but the K&A work and My Higher Power have helped me through that as well.

I had the privilege to interact with Brian Klemmer literally his last weekend on earth, while he was in Albuquerque. I asked him, "Did you have doubts before leaving the military, and pursuing your own business running seminars?" He said to me, "If it's God's will [or a calling to pursue], there is no doubt." He really felt he was walking in his Higher Power's will, and that alone was tremendously inspiring. I probably spent less than 10 minutes with the man, but his words will always be with me. That was worth the price of admission alone. I felt the man (and the program) had two feet on the ground.

Ironically, none of the real benefit would have happened (the sobriety, the continued K&A participation) without going all the way to and through Sam Camp. That's when the lasting change really took place.

I am a courageous, trusting, honest and joyful man
Ray W.
Albuquerque ALS 129, Heart 28, Camp 18

Taylor Hoopii received many breakthroughs and gifts through the experience with Klemmer & Associates. Those gifts are growing and still giving among people in Hawaii who need hope and encouragement.

I was introduced to this work in January of 2011. I attended the Personal Mastery weekend in February of 2011 with Dani, my wife of 20 magnificent years. The powerful self-discovery I made during Personal Mastery determined our decision to also attend the Advanced Leadership Seminar in May of 2011. The Advanced Leadership Seminar was the catalyst behind the "great amount of change" I've created for my life and my future. Klemmer & Associates helped me discover my passion and purpose for changing lives, especially with the youth of today.

Brian Klemmer's influence led me to creating the following successes in my life:

- *The creation of a nonprofit organization, "Ha'awi Mai Ka Pu'uwai" (To Give from the Heart). I am the President of this organization which oversees two impactful projects that help communities struggling with social issues. One project provides education and the spirit of celebration for seniors who have fallen victim to abuse or pedestrian fatalities, the program is called Aloha no na Kupuna (Love for our Elderly). The second project is Project "THINK" (To Help Inspire Neighborhood Kids). This project redirects and transforms the lives of at-risk and high-risk youth involved in delinquency, truancy, drugs, gang involvement, low self-esteem, and a lost sense of direction in their lives.*

- *In 2012, Project "THINK" was selected by the Honolulu Police Department's awards committee as Project of the Year, which led to my sergeant receiving both the 2012 Officer and Sergeant of the Year award for the City and County of Honolulu.*
- *Becoming co-owner of "Time 4 Change Hawaii" with Don Faumuina, a fellow K&A graduate. Formed in September of 2012 as a direct result of Brian Klemmer's influence, Time 4 Change Hawaii has a mission statement that is committed to produce successful results and changing lives through experiential learning, one heart at a time. I now mentor and facilitate workshops based upon a curriculum for champions for all youth. At-risk and high-risk youth are referred by various youth organizations and the judicial system. It is moving and life-changing when incarcerated youth choose to be vulnerable enough to accept love and support from me through our program. That results in them making choices toward positive change.*

I am forever grateful to Brian Klemmer who made me realize that "I am a Committed, Focused, Trusting and Vulnerable Man"

Love and Aloha,
Taylor Hoopii
ALS 155/YLC 21 Staff

As a teenager, Lyse-Anne Cazelais started learning lessons and mastering skills that very few adults ever embrace. All of us strive to make a difference in the world. The sooner we start, the farther we can go.

I attended Klemmer & Associates' Youth Leadership Camp the summer I finished high school. I was planning to start college in September. I was only 16 and had a REALLY BAD high school experience. I had the opportunity to go to YLC. I did not want to go for any of the right reasons...I just figured it would be a fun time in California with a bunch of teens my age...But I was not ready for what was to come my way. A few of the kids just did not want to be there, and disobeyed most of the rules the first two days. I was also very closed off to the experience.

I decided to open up, and as a result, made great friends all over the country (a handful I'm still really good friends with). I grew so much and learned how to deal with my emotions. A teenager arrived in San Francisco the first day...but, a young adult left by the last day.

The kids that disobeyed rules at the beginning of camp were the most grateful for the experience at the end of it.

I went back as Staff the next year, when I was 17. I lived the experience differently. This time, I was extremely proud of how the students progressed and grew so much through the whole experience.

I understand that it is not cheap, but it is extremely worth it. Give your child an experience that could change their lives, their view on the world, and themselves. I know it did for me, and it made me a better person than I could ever have been without it.

Lyse-Anne Cazelais
Youth Leadership Camp 15 and 16

Connor Hoeft demonstrates that what society considers as *normal* teenage traits don't have to prevail in the lives of young people.

Last summer my parents informed me I was going to a Youth Leadership Camp in California. I was very upset and nervous when I found this out, because I wouldn't know anyone and didn't want to spend almost a week of my summer at a camp. Once I got there, after a few short hours, everyone was like a family, offering support and comfort.

Before I went to Youth Leadership Camp, I was argumentative with my parents and siblings. After I came home, I felt more mature. Now I get along so much better with all of my family members. Another great aspect of this camp is that I feel like I have learned a lot about how to have good relationships with people; I give good advice to friends when they are in need. All of the information I learned at this age has shaped me to become a better person now, and in the future! Teenage kids not wanting to go to this is normal, but not wanting to leave is guaranteed.

Connor Hoeft, 14

Heather Seaman had a friend who was willing to take a chance and recommend a Klemmer experience while Heather was still in her teens. If you impact an adult, it can change their world. If you impact a young person, it can touch everyone's world.

I was invited to attend a Champion's Workshop in fall of 2011 by a trusted mentor and friend named Jared Bower. I was 17. Jared gave me a ticket. He told me to go, and then pay him back if I thought it was worth the $20. I went, not because I knew anything about Klemmer, but because Jared had asked me to go. I went with no expectations, whatsoever. Since then, I have been to Personal Mastery,

Advanced Leadership and have committed to going to Heart of Samurai before I graduate from college.

The value I created by attending Klemmer & Associates' leadership training is overwhelming. As a high-achieving and very ambitious individual, I based my self-worth on my ability to perform and meet expectations, rather than on my God-given identity. Though I was raised in a Christian home, I never fully understood this or accepted it until I went to Klemmer.

Through K&A's training I was able to improve communication with my parents, who both later attended a Personal Mastery Seminar. I came to understand how programs had influenced my thinking and behavior. Some of my programs were extremely helpful in moving me forward, but I discovered others that were impeding my ability to form strong relationships.

The most powerful breakthrough at PM was the recognition of how much I judged others. At Advanced, I delved deeper into this and came away knowing that I can only despise in others what I despise in myself. As I continue the journey towards loving and accepting myself more fully, I am able to see others more clearly and remove barriers that once stood between me and my closest friends.

I am currently attending Harvey Mudd College in Claremont, CA, an extremely demanding math-science focused college. Mudders like to say it's the MIT of the West Coast. Since arriving here in August, 2012, I have found that the tools Klemmer gave me are absolutely invaluable. Each day, I face seemingly insurmountable challenges of every sort: intellectual, emotional, spiritual, and physical (I am on the Varsity Swim Team). I no longer embrace "blame, shame or guilt". I practice staying grounded and centered even in the midst of impossible assignments and mountains upon mountains of homework and classes.

After 18 years of small-town life in my hometown of Yakima, WA, the transition to college could have been a very rocky one indeed, but K&A's training allowed me to adapt much more smoothly. I hate to think of how this year could have been had I never attended any of the K&A trainings. Each day is a trial here, and I am learning that the tools certainly do not make life "easy." I am learning to be comfortable being uncomfortable; to face challenges and obstacles with an open heart. I will be the first to admit I have not mastered this yet, but I will keep practicing!

Topics for conversation on campus tend to be those including food, relationship gossip, school, homework, and movies. At the beginning of the Spring Semester, I created a small group that I call my "Dead Poets Society" (ever seen that movie?). I started it because I was starving for a basic essential in my life: deep, serious conversation. I invited a group of girls to join me for an hour of serious conversation once a week on Friday nights. As I hoped, our group of eight have become much, much closer as friends and we've built trusting relationships. As I develop these relationships, I find I use the tools I gained at K&A seminars often in my conversations with them.

In my experience, the majority of students on the college campus are hard-working, highly-intelligent, and ambitious individuals. It breaks my heart to see so many of my classmates who are so brilliant and creative, be completely lost in social settings. Many, many others, and myself included, struggle with perfectionism and lack of self-worth. The bar is set so high here that I can never quite feel "on top of things." Klemmer's training helps me immensely with that, but I would hate to hear the stories others tell themselves when they get their exams back; when they don't sleep for three nights because they're working on homework; when they are betrayed by a friend or significant other or deal with family issues from a distance. At college, I believe so many students are afloat on a sea with no objective standard of right and wrong, or any sense of legacy.

My main breakthroughs with K&A came from the relationship side of Klemmer's training, and I would guess that many other students here would have the same experience. These students will become tomorrow's leaders, whether they are ready to accept that leadership or not. If Klemmer can make an impact on even a few of these people, the results would be far-reaching. Though I never knew Brian Klemmer, this seems to be in line with his vision for K&A. I could write much more about this, but my point is, Klemmer & Associates has a lot to offer this audience and I would absolutely love to help.

Heather Seaman

Most people in this world today are happy with the status quo. Being average seems to be good enough. A few people seek growth and personal development on their own and are willing to stretch to the limits they imagine for themselves.

Brian Klemmer forced me and countless other people to consider a bigger horizon, a larger goal, and a more impactful destiny.

5

Joy and Solutions

As a blind person myself, the biggest challenges are not what you might think. I can deal with not being able to read print, drive a car, or even the challenge of finding my way around a strange city or an unknown stage in an arena or convention center. The biggest challenge I or anyone with a disability faces, is the lack of expectation of other people.

When I met Brian Klemmer, we became both colleagues and friends. It was instantly apparent to me that not only did he expect me to perform like everyone else but expected me to perform at a level higher than I had ever imagined for myself.

Over the years of doing the opening keynote for dozens of Klemmer events, I have met many people with various sorts of disabilities or challenges. I always tell these people, "Don't expect to be normal or be treated normal. Expect to be extraordinary."

My name is Heide Hargreaves. I am a Deaf/hearing-impaired author, speaker and serial entrepreneur. For many years, I was afraid of speaking. I felt (and I was) left out of the hearing world. I was left out of doing things that I wanted to do. I realized that I was getting myself nowhere by trying to change people; trying to get them to take off their different colored sunglasses. I felt tired, frustrated, and upset. I wanted to quit life. I was not feeling good about the people around me. I knew I needed to change something.

I decided to take the opportunity to see if Klemmer & Associates would be willing to help me. The day I took the Personal Mastery course, I was shocked to "see" myself. I decided I would not be a victim anymore. I took the stand that what I believed in my heart and soul was right. Then, unexpectedly, I was able to get other people to take off their different colored sunglasses. All I had to do was change my perspective and to understand where they were coming from.

My most memorable day was at the Advanced Leadership Seminar. I was with my team of 50 people discussing solutions. Apparently there were too many people talking all at the same time and my sign language interpreter had a hard time interpreting multiple voices at the same time. I stepped forward in confidence and I spoke in a loud voice saying "everyone, please, only one voice, one voice!" Suddenly everyone was quiet and listened to me. Wow! That was a new experience for me. It caused a big shift in my thinking. I now feel confident that I can lead a room full of 50 people or more. I took a huge risk. Being out there was like "putting my butt on the line."

Once I got back to Arizona, everyone who knew me noticed a big change in me and told me I was glowing and looked more confident. Some said they couldn't pinpoint what was different, but that it had a good vibe.

I really love Brian Klemmer's concept of "No One Left Out." That speaks strongly to me. I am very thankful for Brian Klemmer, and the company he created. K&A applies the philosophy they promote. Imagine if the whole world could use and apply this concept the way Klemmer & Associates does--there would be peace. Aaaahhh! The bliss it would be!

I am an honorable, wise, confident woman!
Heide Hargreaves

Sandy Park, like many people, began to imagine change in her own life when she saw transformation in someone she knew. Then Sandy had to confront a modern-day reality; that we all seem to know the cost of everything, but the value of nothing.

I first heard about Klemmer & Associates through a close childhood friend. She had posted on her Facebook page that she had just come back from a "life-changing" conference. Since I knew her to be a devout follower of Jesus, I messaged her on Facebook and asked about the conference. The thing that caught my attention was that, in her opinion, it "transformed" her marriage. I had known there were some struggles, and was glad to hear that the conference had been such a blessing for her and her husband. She also mentioned that her niece had attended the conference in the summer and walked away with a confidence that she had never experienced before.

Immediately, I was interested in finding out more about these conferences. I have 3 children ages 13, 15 and 16. My heart's desire is for them to know their identity in Christ and live that full and abundant life in Him. My eldest daughter is one of the most gifted young women I know, but she is plagued by insecurity and perfectionism. After speaking with my friend, I knew that I had to find out more about "Klemmer."

Upon deciding to attend the Champion's Workshop, the Lord put on my heart to invite my dear friend and her husband. We went to the workshop together and then to PM. My friends walked away transformed. They re-introduced themselves to each other, and said that for the first time, they realized they really wanted to get to know the person standing in front of them. It was powerful and I was so blessed to be part of it. My husband also had some major "ah-ha" moments. I was so very proud of him and still am. We have an amazing marriage by the grace of God, and it excites me every day to be on this journey with the love of my life.

At PM, we decided to take the plunge and attend ALS. My husband was more motivated than I was. The greatest gift I received from PM was a confirmation that what the Lord was doing was indeed bearing good fruit. Though very thankful to have been at PM with my husband and dear friends, I didn't know if it was "worth" the investment to move further. And therein lies one of the reasons for my hesitation...money. I tend to be a very generous person with those around me, but very frugal toward myself. So, it was very difficult for me to justify the expense for ALS. In the end, the thing that clinched it for me was my husband's enthusiasm for attending ALS, and the fact that Brian Miller, our facilitator, mentioned that one whole day would be spent on understanding how we relate to money. I knew that I had an issue with money, and decided to go ahead and invest in ALS to see what lurked behind my "money walls."

ALS...the first 4 days: wonderful, eye-opening, humbling. Then came the invitation to attend Heart at the banquet dinner and competing commitments the next day. Once again, my husband was *impressed to continue on with his Klemmer journey and sign up for Heart of Samurai. And once again, I fully supported his decision, but wasn't sure if it was worth the investment for me. We also signed up all three of our children for teen camp...I knew after spending 4 days with Kimberly Zink that I wanted them to experience teen PM/ALS with her. She was an absolute inspiration to me, and I knew that she would be a tremendous blessing to my kids. In the end, I signed up for Heart of Samurai as well.*

The last day of Advanced Leadership I made a commitment to my small group to spend money on myself the same way I would donate to others. This included pampering myself every month (until attending Heart of Samurai) with a massage, facial, and manicure/pedicure. I really struggled with accepting this new commitment, as I did not want to spend money on something that I felt was completely frivolous. My loving and supportive small group came along beside me and just loved on me. They continued to tell me that I was worth it...that I was beautiful, that I was so lovable and so loved. That moment made my entire Klemmer journey worth it for me. It made all the money that I had spent on myself to get there worth it. And it made my decision to continue on to Heart...worth it. It made me realize that I still had some deep-seated wounds surrounding my self-worth. And in that moment, I knew that my God was meeting me there and desiring to uproot those lies and bring me to a place of greater healing and freedom.

I am still on the journey, and I'm not going to stop. I've had amazing "ah-ha" moments with my husband and my kids...and I have regular reminders of where I am and where I want to be. I know to live the full, abundant life God has for me, I need to fully embrace who He has made me to be and step out in faith and do it.

The other day I wrote this on my Twitter, "The more we shrink back from operating in our giftings, the more dim our light becomes. I want to shine as brightly as I can for my Jesus." I thank Klemmer for being stepping stones along the way in my journey, and for bringing alongside me some of the most amazing, incredible, supportive people who I have the great privilege of calling my friends...love you ALS TEAM 170 (and especially group number 1, WE ROCK)!!

Sandy Park

Throughout her Klemmer experience, Joy Moore found a sense of urgency that is critical to all success and happiness. During our years together, Brian taught me this through both his words and his life:

Life is a gift to be savored.

After his untimely death, I will never again be complacent about the hours, days, and minutes we all have been given.

As I reflect back over the different sessions of personal development I attended with Klemmer & Associates, I see how several of the sessions continue to impact my life in a positive way. One constant thought in my mind is: "If I had only six months to live, what would I do?"

I have been living with my daughter's family in Ohio for the past two years. She has twins. I have been the full time "Granny Nanny" and I love being here. I am making another two-year commitment to be here as my daughter is beginning an MBA program. Having a positive and constant impact on the lives of these wonderful grandchildren is a calling that God has placed on my heart. I do not want to come to the end of my life and say, "If I had only...," so here I am. I pray that the stability that I offer will make my grandchildren happier and healthier human beings.

To be centered and to live in the moment has brought me much joy and fulfillment. I have taken away many life lessons that impact my everyday life! Living each day to its fullest is such a blessing. Having no regrets and being able to truly forgive has filled my life with much joy and peace. To be truly "in" is necessary, and I have been able to move into this space completely.

Thank You Klemmer for making such a positive impact on my life!

Joy Moore

For many years, I have written a weekly column entitled Winners' Wisdom. I shared many of these syndicated columns with my friend Brian Klemmer. He gave me a number of ideas and concepts for future columns, and in this way, Brian's wisdom and light went out to countless people through the hundreds of newspapers, magazines, and online publications around the world that carry Winners' Wisdom.

Each of the hundreds of Winners' Wisdom columns ends with a single phrase, "Today's the day!" If Brian Klemmer's life and legacy stand for anything, they stand for the truth that we need to seize the day and seize the moment right now.

Today's the day!

6

Discovery and Success

I remember the fateful day when I gave in and told Brian Klemmer I would speak at just one of his events.

The Samurai events where I do the opening keynotes for Klemmer & Associates are held at Paradise Point Resort in San Diego. It is one of the most beautiful spots in the world. When the tide is up, it is actually an island in Mission Bay. One moment, you're driving along a busy city street in San Diego. Then you turn onto a tree- and flower-lined drive, cross a bridge, and you are in paradise.

After my first experience of speaking at a Klemmer event just to get Brian off my back, I couldn't wait for the next one. To date, I have done dozens of Klemmer events and expect to do many more in the future.

There are many blessings that come from doing the opening keynote for a Klemmer event and being around Klemmer people, but I treasure the memories of the hours I spent with Brian. Several times each year for more than a decade, we sat outside of the meeting room near a picturesque fountain by the marina.

I remember the day Brian turned to me and asked a simple

question. "Do you like yourself?"

I responded affirmatively, and he inquired, "Why?"

I told him about my successful, Emmy Award-winning television network, my best-selling books, the major motion pictures made from my novels, the opportunity to speak to millions of people around the world, and my successful syndicated column.

Brian laughed and responded, "I understand you like what you do, but the question is, 'Do you like yourself?'"

That began a journey of discovery for me that is a part of my ongoing Klemmer experience, much like the revelations experienced by Cris Carter.

Although I followed the typical path of success, college, law school and my own law practice, I wasn't happy, passionate, or fully engaged. Running a successful practice as an attorney and having a lot of influence didn't propel me to become who I really wanted to be. All the education, talents, and skills I used to help others, I also used against myself. I argued, in my mind, all sides of every issue to the point where my inner voice created insecurities that I hid from others. The constant battle kept me locked down and inhibited forward movement.

I had every THING that comes with being successful: waterfront home, several boats, fancy cars, and lavish vacations. Externally, everyone wanted my life. Internally, I knew there was something more. I didn't wake up in the morning with joy. I just existed, going through the motions. Even my relationship with my husband wasn't all that it could be.

The Klemmer experiences helped me understand what was

holding me back. It wasn't easy, but the value was so incredible, that each time I had a breakthrough, I was able to take leaps forward. It was no longer about me pretending or me putting on a demeanor--it was about me knowing who I was and reaching out and connecting to so many other people and resources.

One of the amazing changes is in how I now deal with challenges and problems. Before, I was in attack mode, which was very draining and didn't always get me the result I wanted. I now have all this creative energy to look for solutions I probably would not have seen before. Now I wake up joyful and am excited to see what the day is going to bring. Will it be totally amazing or a fascinating challenge? When there are difficulties, I don't go down to meet them, I now rise above them.

Before, I didn't value relationships beyond my family. Now I am easier to get along with, connect at a deeper level, and have significant relationships with more people. I am no longer an island thinking that I need to do it all myself. Because of these new relationships, my world is more joyful, meaningful, and unlimited. I am so excited to see what each day brings.

Cris Carter

Lorry Leigh Belhumeur discovered, through her Klemmer experience, what we all must learn if we are to be truly successful:

More does not always equal better.

If your goal is to have prosperity with perspective and purpose, resources are great things. But if you just want more for the sake of having more, it is a never-ending rat race, and a futile cycle.

I started on my Klemmer journey less than a year ago. At that time, I had reached a high level of success in my profession, yet I felt stuck; somehow inhibited from achieving more. I was in a self-discovery process when I first heard of Klemmer and was really looking for something that would help me break through barriers that I faced day in and day out. In my Personal Mastery experience, I learned how my own thoughts are often the barriers to my success. That was such a relief, because I have the ability to change my thinking. As a result of Personal Mastery, I now view myself, my relationships, my job, and circumstances very differently. I used to go through life dreading most days. Now, I feel optimistic and look forward to the new experiences I have every day.

I had so many breakthroughs in Personal Mastery. I found it hard to believe there was so much more to learn about myself. Advanced Leadership Seminar (ALS) was a profound experience. I learned more about myself in this week than all the hundreds, if not thousands, of hours spent reading self-help books and attending self-help seminars, workshops, coaching, and mentoring combined. My family, friends, and employees all thank you, Brian Klemmer, for helping me be a much nicer person to be around.

This Klemmer experience has helped me realize I am capable of so much more. I have learned practical ways to create abundance in every way in my life--abundance of joy, relationships, love, honor, etc. This shift has resulted in stronger and deeper relationships, more success in my business, and a much greater positive outlook on what the future holds!

Lorry Leigh Belhumeur

Vicki Voyles was fortunate enough to have a family member that launched her on her Klemmer journey. Through the process, she discovered a bigger family and reminds us all to never wait to take that next step. If you are sitting there contemplating when you should begin a journey with Klemmer & Associates, I have one very good piece of advice: Don't Wait!

I turned 62 years old when my daughter gently nudged (pushed) me into going to a Champion's Workshop and then a Personal Mastery. I discovered things in those classes that I did not want to face. Those discoveries allowed me to change my years of wall-building and let people see my heart.

Then I stepped into the Advanced Leadership Seminar room and met these amazing facilitators led by the most amazing, beautiful woman. She saw right through my stuff. I tried to stay out of her line of sight so she would not see me hiding from life. Well needless to say, it did not work. So I made a "choice" to continue instead of "having" to continue this wonderful experience.

I completed the Heart of the Samurai class with my heart soaring and relieved of a burden I had carried for 24 years. I had lost a husband and a son in those years, but I gained the Klemmer family. I realized there were other people in the world that loved me and that I loved in return.

Samurai Camp was totally amazing, and again, I gained more family members. We cried and loved together while forming a bond that won't be broken, knowing we are always there for each other.

In short, I wish I had allowed this journey to happen when I was 38 years old instead of 62 years old. I lost years of choosing to enjoy my life. If I could have, I would have encouraged more people to take a Klemmer journey of their own, and I know I would have met more wonderful people.

Peace, Abundance and Love,
Vicki Voyles

Stefanie Price began her Klemmer journey on a dismal day when she was in a dismal mood, but as often happens, the process takes over, and we find ourselves enjoying unexpected treasures.

I went to the Champion's Workshop in a HORRID winter ice and snow storm. I went because I had paid for it, and I wasn't going to lose my money. I also had a horrid attitude. We arrived late. I sat there with my arms crossed. I'm sure I rolled my eyes, too. After the Champion's Workshop, I thought maybe this wasn't so bad. So I decided Personal Mastery was sure worth a try. PM was enlightening. Wow, I was so challenged. By this time, my friend and her husband had already done PM and ALS. I saw a HUGE shift in her husband after his ALS class, so I knew I had to go. I attended Advanced Leadership, and I learned more about me during that time than I ever knew I could learn. I went on to attend Heart of Samurai and Samurai Camp.

I have come to realize that I am a worthy woman that accepts myself. I also have come to realize that my worth is not based on what others think or feel. I am much more secure and have learned how to communicate with my husband. Now our marriage is on the road to being the best it can be. I know that life is a journey, and I am sure enjoying the ride! I would encourage everyone of every age to give Klemmer a chance. It just might change your life like it has changed mine, and the lives of so many others.

Stefanie Price

Brian Klemmer taught and modeled the lesson that our own expectations of our future, and forgiveness of our own past, are the beginning points to our destiny.

Jessica Besch encountered those powerful lessons at a Klemmer & Associates event.

My journey with Klemmer & Associates allowed me to identify my deep-rooted unworthiness, and the path to freedom, which was an ultimate surrender to my purpose. My purpose is to love the Lord my God with all my heart, soul, mind, and spirit and to love my neighbor as myself. I'm happy to share that I am walking daily in ultimate surrender to God's will for my life. I have experienced true brokenness and repentance before Him. I have finally forgiven myself and been set FREE because of His finished work on the cross! Thank you all for your love and support!

Jessica Besch

Like many of us, Dean Martini has a spouse and life partner that wanted more for him than he wanted for himself. This gentle (or maybe not-so-gentle) prodding came in the form of Klemmer training.

I'm so grateful to have the opportunity to share my Klemmer experience. I reluctantly acquiesced to my dear wife's "gentle prodding" to attend the seminar. I must admit, my life has forever changed for the best. I now have tools, support, and relationships to catapult me through any endeavor. I now choose to embark on business and family projects I never would have imagined doing before. What I previously thought I didn't care about or seemed impossible has turned into new businesses, and I now have a relationship with my father I never knew after 44 years.

I know I can instantly choose joy versus suffering to playing at bigger and bigger levels. I believe that the greatest gift I have internalized is the sincere ability to forgive--to forgive myself as well as others. It's never too late to choose something different for yourself, because you're worth it. You may not know it right now, but when you attend this training you will.

Dean Martini

James Righter learned the powerful truth that one of the greatest blessings of taking a meaningful journey involves the people who travel with you. This is certainly true of the Klemmer family.

This was a wonderful seminar! The best part was the people, who are partially a result of what Brian Klemmer taught! This seminar inspired me to seek success in my life. It has also helped to spawn new ideas for my upcoming book, "Spiritual Logic." I have just started a third notebook of ideas for this book (in March) and plan to begin the manuscript in May after graduating (B.S. in Accounting) from college. A series of other books will follow. Had I not gone to

Personal Mastery, then I may not have realized the value of these ideas or the impact my life has on others. I think it could be of great benefit for me to become more involved with the ongoing work of Brian Klemmer in my future!

James Righter

Before we determine where we want to go and how we are going to get there, we must honestly assess where we are today. Teena Gowdy came to grips with this through her Klemmer experience and found an accountability partner to accompany her from where she was to where she wants to be.

Through the Klemmer & Associates' seminars I discovered belief systems that weren't serving me. I realized how I was avoiding dealing with situations at work and within myself. Being a creative person, I saw how I had allowed missed opportunities to hinder my progress. I saw how I had given myself an excuse to remain stuck in my life and relationships.

It was after the third day at the Advanced Leadership Seminar in San Francisco, that I was able to say I am, and can be, a very responsible person. I can be loyal to my creative side and use it. I don't have to give up. I can use my gifts. I am very grateful for all I went through and the revelations I received.

Auditing Personal Mastery multiple times in my hometown and reading Brian Klemmer's books have helped me speak out without fear. It has given me understanding on why those fears were there in the first place. Those fears are gone! I also have established a lifelong friend with an accountability partner from the very first Personal Mastery weekend. We see each other three or four times a month.

    Teena Gowdy

    I get countless calls, letters, and email messages from people who have read my books or seen the movies based on my novels. I am always amazed when they describe a lesson or uncover a truth in my own work of which I was not aware.

    I used to think I had been unclear in my writing or the story was vague, but now I know lessons abound, and people can find what they're looking for as a custom-made plan for their future. This is never truer than when people experience the impact of Brian Klemmer and his work.

7

Making a Difference

All of us were created with a specific purpose in this life. No matter what we achieve, what we earn, or what fame and recognition we may enjoy, unless we are pursuing our purpose, we are unfulfilled and cannot fully succeed.

Suzanne Lukasievich encountered her purpose and renewed her vision through Klemmer & Associates.

Before I attended The Champion's Workshop and Personal Mastery Seminar, I had forgotten how to dream. I only knew how to do tasks and get results. After Personal Mastery, I began to dream again and be open to options in life. At Heart of the Samurai, I discovered that I was divinely protected and specifically chosen. I heard clearly my purpose in life: to bring others to Jesus by my everyday example of peace and joy. I am still living that out every day. By being true to myself, I have accepted my mission/ministry in life; to be of assistance to those who have been afflicted by emotional, verbal, mental, physiological mistreatment, and sexual abuse or spiritual neglect. Now I help others discover their dreams, skills, and goals while

I discover mine. God's work is never done, and yet each moment is complete as I step into my true desire in each moment. Living moment by moment, step by step in peace and joy, I learn to rest in Him, reach with Him and enjoy a life worth living.

At Advanced Leadership, I felt a desire to host a Champions and Personal Mastery event in my area so that my friends and family could take part. In 2010, that dream came true as I shared my vision with a team member who supported me. Three of us not only hosted one, but two of each event in my city within a three-month window before attending Samurai Camp. What I gained in knowledge of marketing, networking, recruitment, strategy, teamwork, room context, intentions and more is priceless as I did the work to achieve the results.

Suzanne Lukasievich

Susan Holsinger discovered through her Klemmer experience that in order to build our business, our income, our success, or a life, we must first understand and build ourselves.

The year was 2006. I was working my very first home-based business and my up-line leader suggested I attend courses with Klemmer & Associates to build my business. My husband Philip and I had never heard of Klemmer.

We decided to go to the first course called Personal Mastery in the fall of 2006. We were not prepared for the impact the weekend had on us! We learned the Formula of Champions, the 4 main communication styles, and how to interact with each one of them. We discovered that a large percentage of the decisions we thought we were making were actually made on "auto-pilot." We wanted to learn more and continued on to Advanced Leadership and Heart of the Samurai. We completed Sam Camp in the summer of 2007. During that time, my sales increased seven times and my husband was working with me full-time at home. This was a dream come true for us!

Along the way, I found someone I really did not know as well as I thought I did. That person was me! I found out why I did not really like myself very much and what was holding me back from doing the things that were important to me. I learned to pay close attention to the dialogue in my head, which helped me understand a lot about myself. This new awareness brought many new and different choices. For the first time in my life I was making conscious choices instead of going through the motions and living life on autopilot. My life had purpose and meaning; complete with goals, hopes, dreams, and an action plan to accomplish the things I am committed to!

Since completing all the Klemmer courses, I have written two books and am working on a third one. I started a grief ministry and went through training to be a Certified Grief Recovery Specialist. I currently work with people who are devastated by grief by providing a tried and proven method that helps them say goodbye to the pain that holds them hostage, so they are free to live, love, and trust again.

Another very special thing happened in 2007. I started writing songs...both the words and music.

What I learned through Klemmer & Associates helped me overcome huge obstacles. One very big obstacle: I could write songs in my head all day long...but to put them on paper so other people could actually sing them--I had no clue how to accomplish that! God showed *me He had special plans for the songs He sends. "Holsingers Heartfelt Harmonies" released our first CD in Dec. 2012. We are currently working on another one. Three of our children and myself sing 4-part, gospel harmony with guitar, harmonica, piano, and auto-harp that reminds people of the Chuck Wagon Gang. A song book of all the songs I've written so far is planned, as well as additional CDs. No one I knew had ever done anything like this before. We learned along the way; confident there was a way.*

It was a special privilege to meet Brian Klemmer and have several life-changing conversations with him. At the time, we had no way of knowing how much these courses would change our lives forever! Many people live life without a purpose. Many live without thought of contribution, and take no action to make changes they want to see in the world.

Brian Klemmer at Klemmer & Associates helped us find our purpose and know what to do, once we understood our purpose. Brian's motto is "Creating a world that works for everyone with no one left out."

Why don't you join us and experience K&A's training for yourself? The joy is in the journey and the best time to start is NOW!

Susan Holsinger

John Riverson discovered through a Klemmer experience that to change the world we must change ourselves, and good things will flow from the inside out.

Beginning with a Champion's Workshop, and following up with the Quickening, the K&A courses offered a rare opportunity for me to think and look deep within myself to find who I can be for me, and for the glory of God. It is a journey that has helped me to apply my knowledge and experience in my own personal mastery leadership skills and improve my personal relationships (both of which I considered an element of Christian growth and maturity). The Advanced Leadership Seminar led into Heart of Samurai, which showed me the path to benevolence. Both of the latter enabled me to cast away fear and be bold. I now have a more focused and sharpened purpose in life, applying the full meaning of my faith: "I can do all things through Christ who strengthens me." By the end of the journey, I had written more than 60 pages of a book I always intended to write, but hadn't. My wife Esther and I became more united in purpose and resolve to bless the underprivileged children in Africa through CITA Foundation.

John Riverson

Until we accept the fact that we are responsible for our present condition, we cannot take control of our future success. Tammy Werthem encountered this powerful truth through the teachings of Brian Klemmer.

Gratitude fills my heart for the people who shared their experience with Klemmer, and moved me forward to a Quickening. At the Quickening, I grew in awareness of how I show up in my marriage, as well as in other positions in my life. I gained understanding about how the choices I make, and fail to make, are impacting myself and others in ways I wasn't even aware of.

Choosing to move forward to ALS took some time, and I am so glad I chose to advance. The experiences and life lessons gained from my ALS week will impact me for a lifetime. The clarity and focus that I practiced and brought home will help me build a legacy for years to come. Learning to operate on a team and use my unique gifts reminded me that I have a great contribution to make to humanity.

So grateful for the facilitators who are authentic, trustworthy and bold in helping us all move forward in our lives.

Tammy Werthem

Compassionate Samurai

Esther Riverson was exposed to Brian Klemmer and his message through her church. Brian never separated his faith life from his family life, business life, or personal life. Brian understood that our beliefs are not what we do. Our beliefs are who we are.

I started my Klemmer journey in 2009 when Brian Klemmer visited our church in Springfield, VA, and introduced the Quickening Preview which was going to take place in Alexandria, VA. My husband and I bought our tickets, attended it, and followed it up a few weeks later with the Quickening, a Christian-based version of Personal Mastery. That was a breakthrough weekend for me. I had a complete mind–shift, realizing that it is up to me to take action if I want things to change in my life.

Since then, I have taken the Advanced Leadership Seminar, Heart of Samurai, and now I am finishing Samurai Camp. It has been a revolutionary journey. A journey in change of mind, heart, and outlook in life as I discovered myself and united with the person I have always wanted to be. The person I have become is quite different from the one who started this journey four years ago. Thanks to the visionary, Brian Klemmer & Associates, and thanks to God for ordering my steps and enabling me to take advantage of this wonderful opportunity.

Esther Riverson

I am a committed, focused, and urgent woman. I am filled with joy and kindness.

April Gibson learned through her Klemmer journey that, while change is never easy, it's far better than staying where we are.

What a ride it's been! Nine months of the most intense training on earth. My journey with K&A has been the most meaningful self-improvement journey yet! I never thought I would be able to connect with people in a meaningful way again. And it's pretty easy. I've left behind the pain, victim mentality, shame, blame, and guilt. It is pretty awesome! It's all about choice. Choosing to be happy, peaceful, forgiving, content--it's all a choice. Why aren't we taught this earlier in life? We spend too much time in the resentment, and not enough time on healthy emotional living and connecting with one another.

Learning how to forgive myself was the key to learning how to forgive others. For so long, I allowed others' opinions, moods, wants, and desires to become my own. In a reverse Golden Rule, it's as simple as treating yourself as you would want others to treat you. I have been my own worst critic.

My goals include publishing an NKH information packet and writing a book on sexual trauma; each will contribute significantly to soothe the pain of others, in very different ways. My ultimate goals of establishing a company to fund NKH research and publishing my books to help others are within my reach! Focus, determination, abundance, courage--I will use all of these to my advantage.

I've always been certain of a higher power, and I've been shown how limitless this power is. I will trust in it every day in every way. So many "Ah-ha!" moments. Stepping into the qualities of a Compassionate Samurai has provided so many opportunities for growth. Of all of these growth experiences, and the fact that I've been able to leave many of my lifelong fears behind, shows how far I've come. Can you say SKYDIVING?! I'm so proud of myself!

April Gibson
Sam Camp 24

Suzanne learned that true success is a product of mind, body, and spirit.

I have released approximately 50 pounds. I endeavor towards being physically fit and strong by age 60, so that I continue to trail bike and exercise long into my elder years. I am spiritually sound. I have been able to forgive, trust, and love myself, God, and others. I have gained strong intimate friendships around the world and have close friends nearby that can assist me in my life's journey. I will never be alone. I desire to mentor others and share the biblical truths I have found so that others can be empowered.

Suzanne Lukasievich

Her Klemmer experience taught Rosanna Aragon that how we feel about ourselves is critical to our own success and the opportunity to help others.

I began my K&A journey in 2009. Within six months of attending the workshops, I released 35 lbs. and dropped 6 sizes in clothes. What I learned about myself is immeasurable and priceless. The awareness I now have around how I act and react in situations (personal or business) is incredible, because I know I can choose another way if I want a different result.

Rosanna Aragon
Certified Life Coach
Moriarty, NM

Brian Klemmer's life and work taught me that success is a never-ending journey, and once we have reached a goal, a more significant one will appear in the distance. We always have more things to do and people to encourage. Brian did this as long as he was alive and continues to do this as his ongoing legacy.

8

Life-Changing Decisions

Throughout dozens of Klemmer events over more than a decade where I have given the opening keynote, I've met countless people who have made a decision to change. The variety of decisions made by these individuals represent every area of human endeavor and challenge.

Success is not a one-size-fits-all proposition--it is a custom-made suit. For each of these testimonials, you can imagine hundreds of people who have been impacted by Klemmer & Associates and who are now making a difference for themselves, their families, and their various communities around the world.

The ALS course has completely changed my life in so many different ways. It has created the chance for me to step into my self-confidence, boldness, and forgiveness. I have realized what held me back in the past, and I am now committed to changing my future to make a positive impact on this world.

Margaret Burdick

As the follow up to what I learned in PM, Advanced Leadership has done exactly that. It has helped me advance more successfully into the next phase of my life as a courageous, trusting, honest, worthy woman. I have a greater understanding of my programs and how they work.

Jane Bosman

An amazing, engaging, hands-on experience that provided a safe space for self-exploration and introspection, and gave us (me) the opportunity for growth in ways I've never enjoyed elsewhere (AND I HAVE LOOKED).

Jon Cooney

ALS blew the lid off all my excuses, ripped all my walls down, put away my masks and barriers, and helped me get to my true self. I now understand that the only person I hid from successfully is myself. I gained lots of new friends and headed down on a whole new path.

Phyllis Knoak

I have created people management/leadership curriculum, I have taught executives at Fortune 500 companies, and I've been highly trained, but I've never seen the results like you have delivered. Unlike other seminars, from which I usually only glean nuggets of wisdom, ALS instructors and staff made my great life improve exponentially. This has changed my life and the lives of others. I am eternally grateful *and am preparing for Heart of Samurai. I am a changed man with more passion and purpose than ever.*

Marc Schulman

I am a highly-educated woman who has made some choices that brought undesirable and painful regrets. I never knew why. I've struggled with depression and self-loathing. At ALS I was reborn.

Janice McPherson

ALS was more than I could even imagine. The power I experienced in myself and in the team was inspiring, and I will take this with me to create extraordinary experiences in an ordinary world.

Pamela Zimmer

My experience at ALS was phenomenal! I let go of anger and resentment. Now I am at peace with myself. I discovered I am a courageous, happy, and vulnerable woman!! I trust in myself and others.

Sara Lamb

The experience at ALS pulled trash out of my trash bag, and refilled it with a long-lost good feeling about myself.

Ric Mazey

Any person, in any process in life, can have the experience of a lifetime.

Trennis Baer

This is the most fantastic leadership training I've ever had. I learned tons about myself.

Sharon Russell

Advanced Leadership gave me the key to unlock the door of life and achieve my dreams.

Deborah Coski

This seminar changed my whole outlook. This experience brought out qualities that were just waiting to shine through. I feel as though I landed in a place where angels not only live, but are created.

Julie Gugino

ALS helped me identify where I was stuck and gave me the tools to get unstuck. It was a time of self-discovery and realization. I can now face my fears, overcome them, and push further than I thought possible.

Julia Shadley

I am now aware of what was keeping me from reaching my goals. Now, I can make different choices so I can succeed, instead of staying where I'm at. I found I can be a great mom and have a successful business. I found out that I am worthy. I know how to work through my fears, and I will continue to get better at it.

Karen Satmary

If you're ready to really see yourself and to create your truth, this course works! If accountability and living in community is missing for you, a sample of your life is available here for you to use as a mirror.

Dafna Amir

I realized the power of intention and commitment in a new way. When you are clear on your destination, you don't need to over analyze everything in order to get there in a timely fashion.

Scott Guthridge

I thought I knew who I was walking into ALS. I discovered a courageous, trusting man I didn't know was there. My future is a blank page that is waiting to be written. It will no longer be written by the expectations of others or the vain images I had conjured up in my head in order to shield myself from others.

Paul Fleming

Thank you for a transformational experience. I will use several of the processes to attain my intended results. What a powerful thing.

Collette Larson

Advanced leadership took me by surprise. I've been attending workshops for decades, so I have to say, "Wow!"

Barbara Whiting

In ALS, I discovered my true value as a person. I was vulnerable. I conquered huge fears and anxieties. I feel so blessed to have shared them with team 82. I now have hope in humanity. Our group attained such a miracle. It was beautiful—

Jan Moody

It was great to recognize what's holding me back in life from achieving the things I want, and returning to who I am and who I was created to be. It was an amazing five days.

Laurie Camenzind

I believe ALS has assured me that I am not my results. I am not afraid to move forward in my business and face the challenges ahead. Success is one step at a time, achievable and enjoyable.

Kathy Fiktarz

During the ALS, I stepped in and recognized that I am, and always have been, an unstoppable titan. I realize that the only thing standing in my way is me and my subconscious beliefs. I am experiencing fear even as I write this, which tells me I am in a great place.

    Anthony Brooks

Since I was 16, I have ventured into business, and always with the same result: a great idea, a great start, but never crossing the finish line or earning a dime. That is not so promising in the world of business. I always fell short of my goals and the finish line. After Advanced Leadership, I have created more wealth, and have crossed over the finish line of my goals over and over again. I am seeing more results in the last four weeks using what I learned at Klemmer than I have in the past five years. I have also learned to enjoy working as a team. That has made a huge difference in my life (I never thought I would enjoy this). I have indeed multiplied my capacity to love, lead, create abundance, and experience results. The Klemmer system has been the key aspect to putting myself in action!

      Edgar Carreno
      Cd Victoria,
      Tam. Mexico

Life after The Advanced Leadership Seminar: hee-hee. It has been a great roller coaster ride! I love roller coasters. I noticed that before ALS I was riding the easy rides--you know the rides that don't have height restrictions! I was doing what I thought society was limiting me to and playing it safe. I have taken some chances lately, which have really stepped up my life. I gave notice at my teaching job, to open new doors...which was huge, especially since this was a job that I wanted for four years. My motives and possibilities have changed. I have practiced tithing. I have adjusted my target of friends; letting some out and bringing some new ones in...it has been amazing. I thrive on adventure in my physical life...NOW, I am learning to thrive in my HEART!!

    ~ With Love~
    Cori G.

Over the last half century, I have lived my life as a fully-sighted person, a visually-impaired person, and now for several decades a totally-blind person. Somehow in the process of losing my sight, I captured a vision of who I could be.

Sight is a precious gift, but vision is infinitely more valuable.

When Brian Klemmer twisted my arm to come and speak at just "one" of his events, I had grown accustomed to speaking at huge arena events and business conventions with many thousands of people. When Brian told me there were only a few hundred people at his gatherings, I was dubious. Over the last decade, throughout dozens of Klemmer events, however, I have gained a new perspective.

When I mentally picture my audience at the business

conventions or arena events, I visualize thousands of people sitting in their seats throughout the vast audience. At Klemmer events, I now visualize a few hundred people in the room but thousands of people behind each of them.

As a speaker, I hope to meet people at the point of their need and change their lives. This is something I enjoy doing and will do from now on. However, at Klemmer events, I have the privilege of changing the world-changers. Everyone at Klemmer events is poised to go back into the real world and make a lasting difference for everyone they touch. In this way, the impact is multiplied, and Brian Klemmer's mission and legacy will never end.

I hope to see you at a Klemmer event.

9

In His Words

As an author, columnist, television executive, movie producer, and platform speaker, I have been introduced by world leaders, elected officials, Hollywood luminaries, and all manner of thought leaders. Without a doubt, the most unique introductions I have ever received were those given by my friend and colleague, Brian Klemmer.

After giving countless speeches to millions of people, I have gotten in the habit of always carrying with me to every event, a printed introduction. The master of ceremony or VIP who is giving my introduction needs to do nothing more than to read the paper. I gave scores of these printed introductions to Brian Klemmer without any results.

Brian would invariably glance at the words on the printed introduction, set them aside, and walk onto the stage to speak to those attending the Klemmer event and to introduce me. Often, he would go off into tangents that made sense in his fertile mind that had little or nothing to do with introducing *me*. By the time I got onstage after many Brian Klemmer introductions, I often felt the need to tell the Klemmer attendees my name, who I was, and (hopefully) why I was there.

I never minded this, because Brian's love, sincerity, and respect always shined through. It would, therefore, not be fitting for me to finish this book without allowing Brian Klemmer to address life topics in his own words.

Following is a transcript of words out of the mouth and from the mind of my colleague and dear friend, Brian Klemmer.

Hi, this is Brian Klemmer, founder of Klemmer & Associates. I'd like to talk with you about how you can get un-stuck and how you can make measureable differences in your life and in your business. To make this point, I would like to tell you a story.

Imagine a child that is fishing. I wasn't actually much of a fisherperson until I had kids. They liked to fish, so I would take them, and we would go fishing. So imagine someone is fishing and somebody like me is watching them fish.

The person who is fishing has his fishing pole, his bait, a bucket, and a 12-inch ruler. Now, as they catch a fish, they measure it against the 12-inch ruler. If the fish is smaller than 12 inches, they put it in the bucket. If it's larger than 12 inches, they throw it back into the ocean.

Even a non-fisherperson like me is going to be a bit quizzical, wondering what they're doing, and why they catch a fish, measure it against the ruler, keep the ones smaller than 12 inches, and throw the ones larger than 12 inches away. You would think, "There's something wrong with this picture."

Now, imagine you ask the person who is fishing, "Hey! How come you're measuring them all, and the ones less than 12 inches you keep, but the ones larger than 12 inches you throw back into the ocean?"

Now imagine the person looks at you and says, "Well, it's really very simple. My wife only has a 12-inch frying pan."

This has to be a silly kind of story, right? But it's really an intriguing kind of story.

What I find is that, many times, we all have frying pans for a brain, meaning we have a certain size frying pan--say 12 inches--and if an idea comes to us that's outside our frying pan, that's bigger than what we can think or imagine, we're throwing it back into the ocean. We think it's unrealistic or only a few people can do it. We reject that idea because it's simply bigger than our mind can think.

Well, I can tell you that I want to stretch your thinking so you can have a bigger frying pan and you are able to attract, create, manifest, and build your business, so you can bless more people.

We all have challenges in our lives and in our businesses, and I want to share with you another story about a carrot, an egg, and some coffee.

Some people are like the carrot, because if you drop a carrot into hot water--and this hot water represents a challenge like the current turbulent economic times, difficulties in your marriage, or a challenge with one of your children--if you throw that carrot into the hot water, these people just wilt. Some people are like this. They're doing just fine in their business and in their life until something comes along that is a challenge, and they just wilt. They collapse under the pressure, so to speak.

Other people are like an egg. And if you imagine an egg, it's got this nice hard shell, and if you throw it into hot water, it doesn't wilt, but the inside of the egg gets hardened. And some people are like that. They get thrown into tough times, and the inside of them gets hardened. They stop being a compassionate, caring person and forget that the real reason for being in business is to provide a blessing for people and to make a difference. So they become hard and calloused and jaded on the inside.

This is a leadership company. What we want is to have leadership over ourselves and then with other people. We want to be more like the coffee. When you throw coffee into hot water, what happens? All the water changes! It becomes coffee.

So when leaders are placed in difficult circumstances, they change the circumstances. So, that's what we do. We train people to be the leader who can handle any circumstance, any time. We call them Compassionate Samurais. That's the title of my number one business book from 2008: The Compassionate Samurai. It's not the violent side of the samurai. It's the idea of being a producer, yet having your whole life be about service.

Even in providing this service, we all need to know how to face problems and solve challenges.

Here's another interesting thought for the day: Do dogs like bones? Most of you are laughing and saying, "Yeah, yeah, dogs like bones."

I'm going to suggest that dogs do NOT like bones. They like steak, and they just settle for bones. You don't have to believe me. Just go borrow a dog if you don't have one of your own. You put a steak out there, and you put a bone out there. Come on...which one do you think he's gonna go for?

Or how about visualizing this? This is a funny picture! Imagine that the dogs were setting the table. I mean, they have the skirts on and the trousers on, they put the silverware out, they're setting the table, and they're putting the meal out there. Who do you think is going to end up with the bones? I think we will, and they'll keep the steak for themselves.

It's not that dogs dislike bones. It's that they settle for bones. I think what happens is that they get fed bones, bones, bones, bones, bones, and they begin to say, "I think I like bones." They simply settle for bones rather than going for steak.

I thought I'd tell that story because some people have a certain level of success in their business life or a certain level of success in their marriage. You know, sometimes if you have a good marriage year after year after year--like good marriage, good marriage, good marriage, good marriage, good marriage--you begin settling for a good marriage instead of creating a spectacular marriage. I'm not talking about changing your spouse, folks. I'm talking about taking the one you're with and making it more spectacular.

Or maybe you've got a certain level of success in your business life and your growth has been kind of flat. But it's good compared to other people, so you've been settling for that good instead of creating that spectacular.

What I'm about with individuals and companies through my company (www.Klemmer.com) is about creating spectacular for people. We're actually the only company that measures the income and activity of people before and after they come and work with us. So, we look forward to working with you as you face your challenges and

The need for leadership in the world:

- 50 percent of people in the world do not have clean sanitation water
- 20 percent do not have adequate shelter
- 33 percent go to bed hungry each night
- 3 percent die of hunger every year
- 70 percent are unable to read
- Only 1 percent are college educated

It does not have to be this way. The need for mastery is urgent. As you fulfill your own dreams, you make a difference in the world around you. When you become a master of life, you have the power to affect the lives of others in unimaginable ways!

Will you do it? Will you make a commitment to get your life in shape? Will you make an agreement to follow the plan for the next ninety days? The eagle in you is calling. Your dreams are calling. Start the exciting journey right now!

To Reach Klemmer & Associates:

Phone: (707) 559-7722
Toll Free: (800) 577-5447
Fax: (707) 762-1685

www.klemmer.com
mastery@klemmer.com
www.facebook.com/klemmer.associates
www.PersonalMasteryBlog.com

KLEMMER & ASSOCIATES
The Premier Leadership & Character Development Company

Go to www.klemmer.com to watch our FREE one-hour Champion's Webinar and receive a special discount for a Personal Mastery Seminar. To view, go to Workshops, click on Champion's Webinar and click on "Watch the Recorded Version." Or to participate in a live webinar, choose an upcoming date, and click Go!

You will learn the Secret Formula of Champions: a Million Dollar formula that thousands of people use to solve problems and create more success in their life – personally and professionally! Create spectacular results when you have NO idea what to do!

Motivating! Inspiring! Life-changing!
Books by Brian Klemmer

You are excited, but it didn't go as planned! 10 ways to get unstuck!

Paperback 144 pages
$14.95 each, 5+ for $8.00 each

The truth is, how-to's are not enough! Find the answers you really need that will get you what you really want!

Paperback 160 pages
$14.95 each, 5+ for $8.00 each

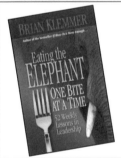

Are you the leader you can be? Learn from a leader of leaders...in 52 bites...how to be a better leader!

Paperback 192 pages
$14.95 each, 5+ for $8.00 each

A Compassionate Samurai is a bold, ethical, results-producing person who makes a difference for others as well as themselves. Learn the traits of a compassionate samurai.

Hardcover 245 pages
$24.95 each

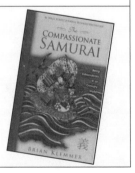

To order, visit www.klemmer.com or call toll-free 800-577-5447

Champion's Workshop

The Champion's Workshop is a two-and-a-half-hour fun, impacting, and experiential workshop based on the "Formula of Champions." Brian Klemmer has interviewed Olympic world record holding athletes, CEOs of major corporations, and successful people of all walks of life in an effort to find the common denominators and keys to success. *The Formula of Champions is the result!*

Have you ever wanted something but were stuck because you didn't know what to do? *Never again! Here is a formula for producing results when you have no idea what to do. You can put this to use immediately.*

Is there a gap between what you want and what you actually get? *Learning why what you want has nothing to do with what you create.*

Present the postcard inserted in the back of the book and you can attend for FREE! This power-packed, riveting workshop is one of many workshops offered by Klemmer & Associates worldwide. Regularly $59!

If you need further information, call 800-577-5447
or visit **www.klemmer.com**.

The Compassionate Samurai Lives On
is proudly published by:

Creative Force Press
Guiding Aspiring Authors to Release Their Dream

www.CreativeForcePress.com

Do You Have a Book in You?